ICE AGE™
Dawn of the Dinosaurs

THE ESSENTIAL GUIDE

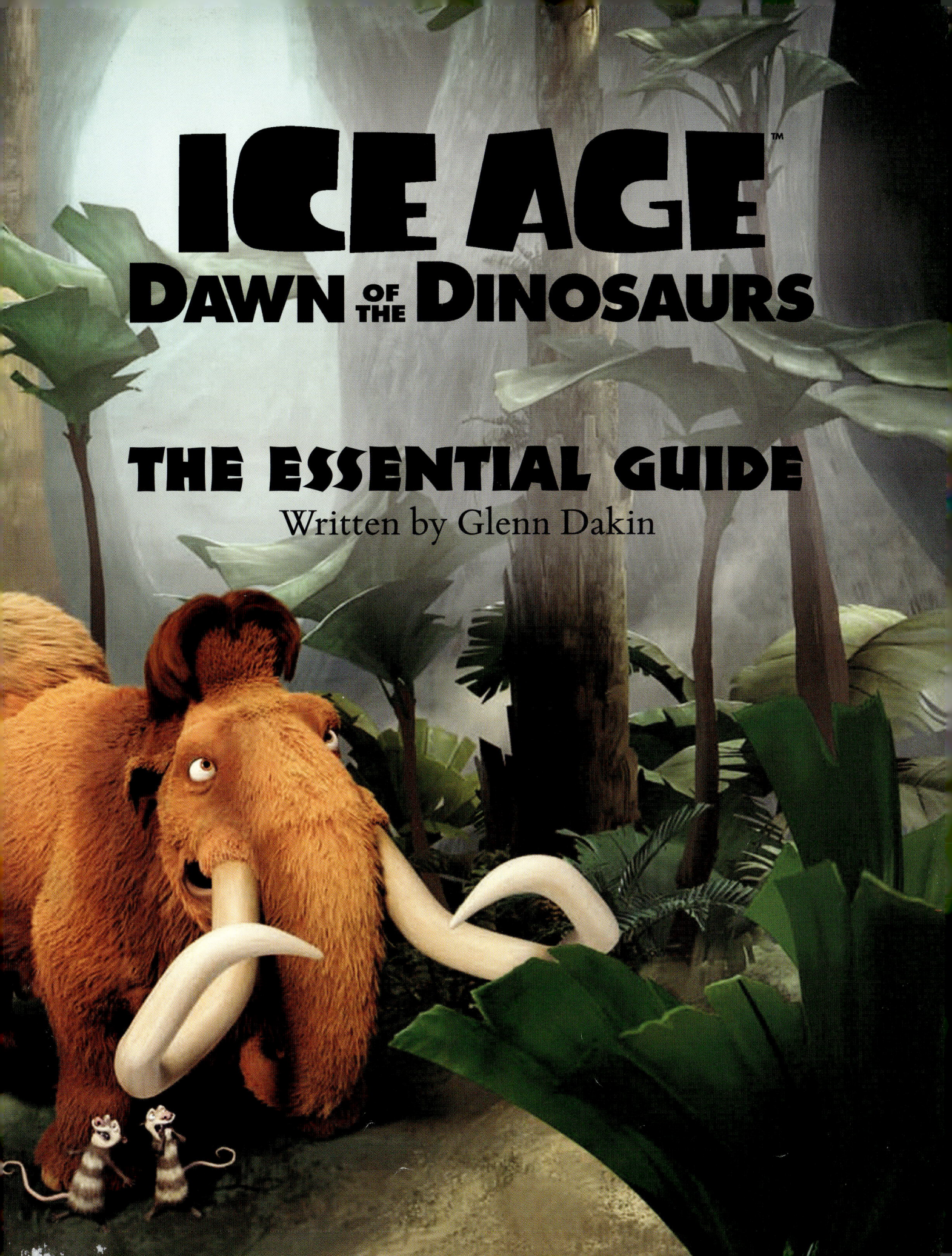

CONTENTS

Introduction	6
The Herd	8
Manny	10
Diego	12
Diego's Top 5 Scary Moments	14
Sid	16
Evolution	18
Ellie	20
Mammoth Love	22
Crash & Eddie	24
Extinct Factor	26
Reptiles	28
Sabre Showdown	30
Dino Kids	32
Manny's Playground	34
Sid's Parental Guide	36
Secret World	38
The Jungle	40
Buck Wild	42
Mamma Dino	44
New Daddy	46
Scrat	48
Scratte	50
Crime Scene	52
Teamwork	54
New Mummy	56
Peaches	58
Family Album	60
Happy Ending	62
Acknowledgements	64

INTRODUCTION

Welcome to the Ice Age, a time when the most amazing creatures shared the Earth – and ate each other for lunch. Blizzards raged, volcanoes rumbled, dinosaurs rampaged – and that was on a quiet day. But in this wild and dangerous time, the greatest friendships were formed and the funniest times were had. So wrap up warm and take your first step into the coolest epoch of all. But be warned, there's something lurking underneath the ice…

THE HERD

Meet the family! Here's the strangest herd that ever hit town, a bunch of close friends who appear to have nothing in common. But they are united by one thing — a strong feeling that the others simply couldn't survive without them!

Ellie
This brave lady mammoth — and part-time possum — is about to become a mum. But when her herd is plunged into peril, she has to stand up to her mate, Manny, and show that being pregnant doesn't mean being left behind!

Diego
Diego the sabre-toothed tiger is worried that there's no place for a ferocious feline in a herd that's more interested in babies than fun. Proud Diego decides to go it alone — until an old pal needs his help…

Manny
This mighty mammoth was once a stubborn loner, but Manny is now taking his role as a family man a little too seriously! His life is made even more complicated by his buddy Sid, who is harder to keep out of trouble than his new family could ever be!

Crash & Eddie
These two possums, Ellie's 'brothers', dice with danger just for fun. But when Sid is sloth-napped, they have to show they can face peril for the sake of someone else.

Sid
Sid the sloth is not happy when the old gang seems to be breaking up. He decides to create a new herd, and he does it in the craziest way imaginable. Didn't anyone ever tell him not to play with dinosaur eggs? Soon it isn't just Ellie who has to face up to the challenge of being a new mummy...

MANNY

He may look like the biggest, grouchiest heap of fur you've ever seen, but underneath all that attitude, Manfred, (also known as Manny), is a woolly mammoth with a sweet, caring nature. Manny was once a loner, but now he has a herd of crazy buddies to take care of, plus a bouncing baby on the way – which surely means more mammoth-sized problems ahead.

The three amigos
Manny is the most loyal friend any creature could hope for. His pals mean the world to him. But there are limits – no way would he trust Sid to do the babysitting for him!

"I'M THE BIGGEST THING ON EARTH!"

Mammoth strength
It's handy having a powerful pachyderm like Manny around when it comes to building shelters – or even making an amazing adventure playground for his newborn baby.

Floppy tail

Earth-shaking feet

Pouffy hair can impress lady mammoths

DID YOU KNOW?
The name mammoth comes from the Siberian word for 'earth burrower'. People thought mammoth remains found in the frozen ground had come from underground.

Out of time?
It's a dangerous world out there and there's a nasty rumour that mammoths are heading for extinction. Manny is fighting back the best way he knows how – by starting up a new herd.

Extra-long tusks – up to 5m (16ft)

Trunk acts like an extra finger

The grouch
Manny is a sensitive guy, especially when it comes to his weight. But as he keeps on telling Sid, he's not fat, it's all his fur – it makes him look pouffy.

11

DIEGO

Once a top tracker for one of the fiercest sabre-packs on the ice, Diego is now a reformed character. Hanging out with Manny and Sid has taught him the value of friendship — and of not necessarily eating everyone you meet. But now Diego is worried that he's going soft. Will he have to leave his pals in order to find his edge?

Sabres have short tempers and long canines! They especially don't like to be reminded of their weaknesses, as Sid soon finds out.

Large eyes — great night-vision

Scaredy-cat
Sabres just don't 'do' water, and the bigger the cat, the greater the scaredy-cat! Sid tells Diego to think of the water as his prey, which seems to help.

Sharp canines used for stabbing prey

Guy issues
When Diego admits he's thinking of going solo again, Manny takes it personally. He thinks Diego just doesn't want to hang out with a bawling baby mammoth.

DID YOU KNOW?
Sabre-toothed cats could grow fangs up to 20cm (8 inches) long. They liked to live in packs and hunted deer, bison, elk, ground sloths and even mammoths!

"I'M NOT A KITTY-CAT, I'M A SABRE."

Diego's dilemma
When Diego is out-run by a gazelle, he starts to feel that he may have to leave the herd in order to stay sharp. But he soon learns that some of life's biggest adventures can happen to you right at home.

.... Manly ruffled-up fur

DIEGO'S TOP 5
SCARY MOMENTS

Sabre-toothed cats don't expect to feel terror – they expect to dish it out. But daring Diego has to face more than his share of terrifying trials when he gets mixed up with Sid and Manny. Like all cats, he has nine lives and usually manages to survive by a whisker.

4

Lava leap
Diego makes the leap of his life when the gang nearly get their fur fried at Volcano Pass.

5

Ice scream
Sure-footed felines always land on their feet – unless they're on an ice slide. This frozen flume ride is so cool, Diego wants to go back for round two!

3. H2O horror
When the ice starts to melt, Diego has to confront his worst fear – water. He can't swim to save his life but he'll give it a try to save someone else's, especially if it's Sid. Diego has learnt that fear is okay – in fact, it's what keeps a cat alive.

2. Cat fight
Face to face with his old pack-leader, Soto, Diego refuses to turn tail, and helps save Manny from a mauling. The fight is nearly Diego's last…

1. I-think-they-saurus
When you're the heroic type, sometimes the hardest thing to do is…nothing! Diego can only watch as two aquatic dinosaurs, Maelstrom and Cretaceous, try to turn Manny into fish-food. But Diego manages to face his fear and save his pals.

SID

Sid the sloth is the stinky, but loveable, glue that holds the herd together. Often lazy, slightly crazy and never far from trouble, he somehow manages to be strangely hard to live without.

Sid attempts to look like a sabre-toothed tiger with the use of two twigs. But he ends up looking more silly than scary.

"I'M GOOD AT MAKING FRIENDS. I'LL MAKE MY OWN HERD."

Foul fur, discoloured by fungus

Poor eyesight – unable to spot trouble coming

Herd mentality
When his old gang appear to be breaking up, Sid is brokenhearted. Nothing means more to him than having his close pals around – who he can irritate on a deeply personal level. It's what he does best. Maybe it's time to start a new herd?

Short, useless tail

Making enemies
Rhino's are pretty thick-skinned, but even their finer feelings can be hurt — especially when Sid wipes his muddy feet in their delicious salad. Carl particularly resents Sid hanging onto his fearsome horn while he does so.

SLOTH FACT!
Sloths are famous for only moving when it is absolutely necessary, and are named after one of the traditional 'seven deadly sins'.

Cracking up
Poor Sid knows what it's like to be abandoned, so when he stumbles across three giant eggs, he decides to be their mummy. Uncle Manny isn't impressed. Whatever Sid is up to, there's going to be trouble!

Sharp claws for self-defence — and picking his nose

17

EVOLUTION

Frozen in this glacier, the development of Sid-kind has been captured forever. The incredible change from brainless blob to the Sid we all know and love is there for all to see. But has much really altered? The first creature looks slightly brighter than Sid does now. So much for evolution…

Without limbs, ideas or purpose of any kind, Sid's lazy ancestors were truly happy – doing nothing.

This aquatic Sid prototype was advanced enough to annoy strangers with its goofy looks.

This recent relative developed broad, powerful arms and used them to wipe his nose on.

Fully evolved, the Sid we all know has learnt to become just as slothful as his first ancestors! But he does have a few more friends…

ELLIE

This mammoth mother-to-be has the toughest job in the world, coping with moody Manny, and trying to keep her batty brothers out of trouble. But there's one thing you can depend on – Ellie will risk her own hide to keep her wacky herd together.

Adopting Ellie
Adopted by possums when separated from her herd in a blizzard, Ellie lost all memory of her original family. She grew up believing she was a possum – despite a disastrous incident when one of her uncles tried to give her a piggyback ride.

Coarse outer hair

Fur-coated ears

"TALK TO THE TRUNK!"

Ellie's crazy upbringing has left her with an unusual skill-set for a mammoth. She can climb trees, hang by her tail and play dead to avoid being carried off by birds.

Family matters

Ellie's bonkers brothers turn her world upside-down on a daily basis with their mischievous sense of fun. Ellie often stands up for them in public, and is always ready to hang them upside down at bedtime. Under all the sibling sarcasm, they are a close and affectionate clan.

Crash and Eddie love to advise Ellie on her personal life and give Manny a tough time when he and Ellie become a couple. If the big guy upsets Ellie, then as far as the possums are concerned – he's extinct.

Broad 'lips' on tip of trunk, for picking things up

Brave Ellie

Her possum side tells her that being brave is just dumb, but Ellie can't help standing up for herself and her herd. When Manny orders her to stay out of trouble, she tells him to "talk to the trunk"!

DID YOU KNOW?

A female mammoth carried its baby for twenty-two months – before giving birth, leaving dad plenty of time to get the playground ready....

MAMMOTH LOVE

This colossal couple might look like they're made for each other, but in fact they got off to a very bad start. Ellie told Manny that mammoths were dumb because they always placed themselves in danger, and Manny couldn't believe he'd met someone as stubborn as, well…himself.

Playing possum

As a potential mate, Ellie has one serious hang-up – she thinks she's a possum! When Manny points out that she has the same footprints as him, she thinks that he must be part possum too! But Ellie soon realises that she was a mammoth all along.

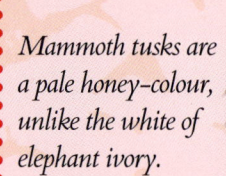
Mammoth tusks are a pale honey-colour, unlike the white of elephant ivory.

The only way that Manny and Ellie can save the whole gang from a fatal plunge is to lock trunks and make up. This scene would be touching if it wasn't so terrifying!

Charmed

Romance is a tricky area for Manny. He can't help getting trunk-tied when he talks to Ellie. But he does manage to charm Ellie by telling her she has a really huge butt. Ellie soon decides that Manny is definitely possum enough for her.

Long tusks can make hugging difficult!

MAMMOTH FACT!

Mammoths did like to live in herds, but it is thought that only the females enjoyed company. The bull males were more solitary creatures, like Manny!

CRASH & EDDIE

These frenzied fur-balls will do anything for kicks. They'll try any crazy dare as long as the other one is there to scrape them off the floor afterwards. But they both know that whenever they push their luck too far, their big sister Ellie will always be there to help them out.

Thumb-like toe gives super grip

Eddie
Eddie is Crash's wing-man of mayhem. He's also the one who wets his bed. Or sometimes Crash wets it for him. A master of torture by pea-shooter, this pesky possum's favourite pastime is rolling in the dung patch.

First impressions
At first the batty brothers don't see eye-to-eye with Diego but they warm to him when he tells them he'll never surrender. That's the kind of attitude they dig.

Eddie has a face-stripe and a pointy nose

Tongue is usually out and used for pulling faces

Crash

Crash loves spectacular stunts — especially if they go wrong. He looks up to Buck and can't wait to get an eye-patch just like his hero. He's sure that deep down, Manny and Ellie's new arrival will be a possum at heart.

Big eyes for night-vision

Crash has a rounded nose

Tail for hanging yourself upside down at bedtime

DID YOU KNOW?
Possums 'play dead' and lie still in the face of danger. This tactic can save them, as it shows a larger animal they do not mean to be a threat.

After their clash with the possums, Sid and Diego pretend they were ambushed by a swarm of rattlesnakes.

Daring duo
They might play dead at the sight of Mamma Dino and tremble at the mention of rampaging Rudy. But that doesn't stop the possums trying their paws at pterodactyl riding!

25

EXTINCT FACTOR!

You may know how to hunt, where to graze, or who to avoid when it's dinner time, but sadly you could still end up on nature's hit list. Let's take a look at some of the Ice Age folk who may be unlucky enough to have…the extinct factor! (Note: a high score means you are more likely to become extinct).

Frank might be a big tough rhino but that doesn't mean he's got what it takes to stay alive. Dining on fresh salad and exquisite flowers may show refined tastes, but can a fussy eater survive hard times? **6/10**

Food glorious food is all these sneaky scavengers think about. In a time of disaster, vultures do well – they just eat up everybody else. Waiting around for your lunch to die first is the hardest part! **2/10**

Plump, easy-to-spot and simple-minded, this dizzy diatryma bird looks like a ready-to-eat lunch. However, those big feet are tricky to swallow, so predators might steer clear. **4/10**

Beavers work hard to stay alive, but this one-horned variety are prone to bad habits (see picture). Interrupting a mammoth during story-time is not a great survival tactic either. **5/10**

26

These saw-toothed snack-lovers eat first and ask questions later. The pirahnas' only problem is choosing their prey. They just don't have the numbers here to take on a hungry scrat!

3/10

Kung Fu skills won't help if you're losing your melons – and your marbles! Dodos have no problem with extinction at all – they're experts at it. Doom on you!

10/10

This cute little mammal is called a start. You might notice they aren't around today. So don't start something you can't finish.

9/10

This ox may lack brains, but her husband assures her she makes up for it in good looks. As for floods, hard times and hungry days ahead, that doesn't scare her – she's always wanted to lose a few kilos!

3/10

This artful armadillo is a fast talker with a tough shell. When it comes to the crunch, Fast Tony could talk his way out of anything – even extinction!

2/10

This ravenous reptile was king of the seas once, but has hung around past his eat-by date. In fact, this irritating ichthyosaur ought to be extinct already. Hurry it up, pal, it's someone else's planet now!

8/10

27

REPTILES

WARNING! HIGH SURF!

It's been a long time since these marine monsters ruled the Earth, but now the big thaw has brought them back to life and there's a treat waiting for them. While the dinos were taking time out, the Earth has been overrun by a bunch of juicy mammals. Look out, Ice Age, it's chow time!

Ridge of protective spikes

Maelstrom

This spiky customer has a jaw like a steel trap, and a brain so small it can hold just one thought: "Let's eat". Maelstrom has had thousands of years between meals and is now ready to make up for lost time. This is not the best time to be swimming!

NAME: Maelstrom
TYPE: Ichthyosaur
EATS: Fish, squid, shellfish and anything else that falls into the water
HABITAT: The sea
STATUS: Extinct

REPTILES AHEAD

Flippers for extra speed

28

Cretaceous

Don't be fooled by his stupid grin – Cretaceous is actually a lot dumber than he looks! He must be, when you consider he has a slow-moving buffet of docile Ice Age creatures to snack on and he tries to get his gnashers into a tough-guy like Manny!

THAW WITH CARE!

Mighty jaws
Short neck
Cone-shaped teeth

DANGER — CAUTION SLIPPERY

NAME: Cretaceous
TYPE: Pliosaur
EATS: These eating machines were so hungry they sometimes ate each other!
HABITAT: The sea
STATUS: Extinct (phew!)

Stu

Slow-witted Stu becomes the first victim of these hungry horrors. An attack of the monster munchies brings an end to his career as sidekick to con-artist Fast Tony. Still, at least Tony manages to ride to safety on Stu's empty shell!

DID YOU KNOW?

Pliosaurs could grow as long as 15 metres (50 feet). That's bigger than a London Bus!

"GOOD SUSHI!"

29

SABRE SHOWDOWN

In the race for survival, coming second is not an option. For a sabre-toothed tiger, if you lose your edge, then you lose your lunch – and your comfy place high up in the food chain. An embarrassing encounter with a gazelle forces Diego to take a look at himself – and he doesn't like the fat cat that he sees…

Sabres have short bob tails

Adios amigos

Diego thinks he has gone soft and only a spell alone on the wild plains will bring back his sharpness as a hunter. Sid is so shocked by this, that he makes a major life decision of his own. In fact, Sid starts off a chain of events that just might bring everyone back together again.

DINO KIDS

The moment they hatch out of their shells, these eager little dinos look to their mum to teach them what to do. The only problem is, the first person they clap eyes on is Sid! When Mamma Dino turns up, the poor little predators get caught in a bizarre tug-of-love. But as long as they grow up to be big terrifying dinosaurs, everyone will be happy.

Shell shocked
Kids can be hard to look after, even before they're born. Sid takes Shelly and Egbert for a trip and ends up doing a juggling act.

All new Sid
Becoming a new mummy brings out a whole new responsible side in Sid. But would a good mummy really take somebody else's eggs? Manny has his doubts.

This dino can be identified by its blue eyes

Sid strikes confident pose – which may not last long!

Food fight

Parents often squabble about what's best for their kids, and Sid and Mamma Dino are no exception. Mamma brings home a flapping, feathery archaeopteryx for lunch, but Sid prefers a healthier vegetarian option. Sid also points out that if Mamma eats him, it'll send a bad message to the kids.

These playful youngsters can sometimes get a bit rough with other kids, which lands Sid in trouble with their parents. Sid is shocked. Don't people realise how tough it is being a single mother of three?

Third dino has lighter eyes and colouring

Second dino has darker brown markings

DINO FACT!
Baby dinosaurs are known as hatchlings. Many were born in nests and first fed by their parents.

33

MANNY'S PLAYGROUND

Scowl reveals he is not impressed with Sid's parental skills

With its vine swings, ice slides, turtle-shell roundabout and obstacle course, Manny's playground is a mammoth feat of Ice Age construction. The proud father can't wait for the day he can see his own kid playing in it. The problem is, everyone else wants a go too, and it isn't long before Manny's playground is turned into a battleground…

Playtime soon turns into terror-time when the dino kids take over Manny's playground. Sid quickly discovers that disciplining three dino kids is not going to be easy!

Manny's law

Manny has to lay down the law and tell Sid his kids just aren't welcome. After all, eating children is not acceptable behaviour in any playground.

Dino kids have rows of savage teeth

Playing nice

The dinos quickly take over the park and behave like little monsters. One dino refuses to share a stick with a beaver girl. Another dino takes things a little too far and swallows an aardvark boy whole. Still, Sid has heard you should let your kids eat what they like...

DID YOU KNOW?
Although mammals and dinosaurs did share the Earth at the same time, there is no evidence that many of them shared playgrounds!

35

SID'S PARENTAL GUIDE

DO

Get used to multitasking. Your role as a parent calls for it.

DON'T

Attempt to juggle three dino eggs at once. You'll only end up with egg on your face.

DO

Try to find out why the baby is crying. Remember, humans are disgusting. It might have a poopy nappy.

DON'T

Hold the baby upside down. You just get the smelly end nearer your face.

DO

Give your child a sense of fun. It's hilarious if you can lob a snowball at your mammoth pal and blame it on the kid.

DO

Remember that babies have no sense of danger – always protect them, especially if you have no sense either.

DON'T

Ever compete with your baby in performing reckless stunts. They are the champs.

DON'T

Be surprised if the kid squeals on you, and you get splatted in revenge.

Responsible, loving and nurturing. Sid likes to think he's all of these things, although others would disagree. But that doesn't stop him having a go at being a parent. Whether it's a pink, squashy human baby, or a bunch of cute dino kids, Sid just loves showing them who's the mummy.

DO

Take your kids out and give them plenty of exercise. If you've found dino eggs, you don't need to wait till they're hatched – they can roll around and enjoy themselves while they're still in the egg! Actually, they're easier to handle at the shell stage, so make the most of it. They grow fangs real quick.

DON'T

Be frightened to give them names before they hatch. For example, Egbert, Shelly and Yoko are all egg-cellent choices! You could even give the eggs their own personalities by drawing faces on them.

DO

Make sure they have a secure environment. Hanging out with a mammoth and sabre-toothed tiger sure keeps away the predators!

DON'T

Give them the best spot at bedtime. Human babies will sleep anywhere, even curled in a stinky mammoth trunk. Save the nice hard rock for yourself to curl up on.

SECRET WORLD

Take a peek into another world…if you dare!
When Sid is snatched by Mamma Dino, the herd set out to look for him and find themselves in a perfectly preserved Jurassic jungle. It might sound like a world of wonder, but to anyone venturing inside, it's a place of dread as it contains hungry dinosaurs, terrifying pterodactyls and mammoth-eating plants.

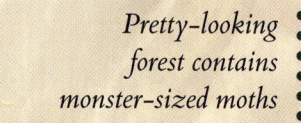

Pretty-looking forest contains monster-sized moths

On the brink of a perilous mission, Manny decides if he ever saves Sid, he's going to kill him.

Sid first drops into this hidden world while admiring his own reflection in the ice.

Lava falls – this is where the dinos care for their newborn babies.

Lava fields – a good place to avoid Rudy, as his weight cracks the ground here.

Pterodactyl nests – if you tumble over the falls, you might want to hitch a lift.

Manny wanted to keep Ellie safe – now they've ended up in the most dangerous place in the world. But at least they're together.

THE JUNGLE

Pouffy hair can stand on end when faced with scary dinos.

Abandon hope, all ye who enter here. At least that's what tour guide Buck says about this prehistoric forest. And if you've lost a friend in here, then they're sure to be found…in the afterlife! So it's doom, despair and a hopeless task for Manny and his herd. But, hey, that's never stopped them before…

"NOWHERE TO HIDE, TERROR EVERYWHERE!"

Fluffy topknot

Wide-eyed terror at seeing jungle for first time

Buck Wild
Surrounded by deadly dinos, the gang are rescued by a wacky warrior — the ever-resourceful rodent, Buck.

Mammoths have smallish ears, perfect for hitching rides on.

Chasm of Death
To find Sid, the herd have to get across an awesome death-drop. The good news is, there's a plate-bone gondola to help you. The bad news is, it emits a toxic gas that has some very funny effects!

JUNGLE FACT!
Cycads, similar in appearance to palm trees and ferns, were common in the Jurassic jungle.

BUCK WILD

Are you ready for adventure, danger and extreme craziness? Then get ready to hang out with the brave Buckminster. This wily weasel of the woods can survive any peril, with everything but his sanity intact!

Machete made from one of dino Rudy's fangs

Mad glint in eye – result of too long spent alone in jungle

Eye patch made from jungle seed pod – necessary thanks to Rudy.

Jungle vine rescue ropes

"RULE NUMBER 1:
ALWAYS LISTEN
TO BUCK."

DID YOU KNOW?

Weasels are great survivors, coming from the mustelidae family of creatures. This family includes feisty ferrets, stinky skunks and warrior-like wolverines!

Long feet and sharp claws means Buck never loses his grip (except on reality).

Rudy

This deadly dino is Buck's arch-enemy. He always keeps an eye out for him – and one eye is all Buck has got left – thanks to Rudy!

Buck loves telling far-fetched tales of his own escapades. Just don't believe the part about the time he was killed…

Buck's rules

So, you want to survive in the jungle? Then you have to follow Buck's rules. Rule one: always listen to Buck! Rule two: stay in the middle of the trail. Rule three: if you have gas, you have to travel at the back of the line. Of course, not everyone likes taking orders from a weasel. After all, who wants to be bossed about by a nutcase who talks to rocks and uses dinosaur skulls as puppets?

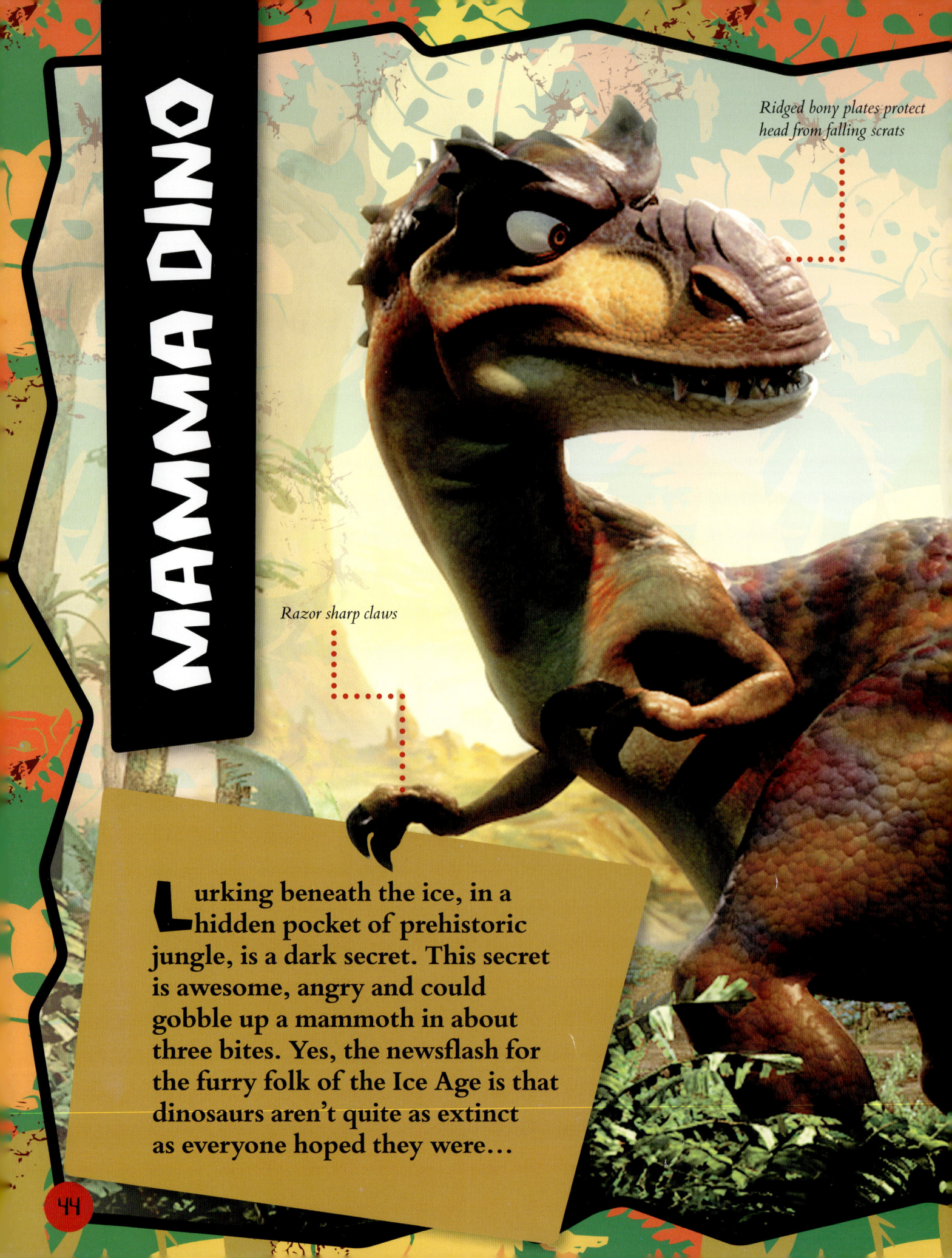

MAMMA DINO

Ridged bony plates protect head from falling scrats

Razor sharp claws

Lurking beneath the ice, in a hidden pocket of prehistoric jungle, is a dark secret. This secret is awesome, angry and could gobble up a mammoth in about three bites. Yes, the newsflash for the furry folk of the Ice Age is that dinosaurs aren't quite as extinct as everyone hoped they were…

Scrat holds on for his life... and his precious acorn

Camouflaged skin allows Mamma Dino to blend into the jungle surroundings.

Mamma mia

As if a rampaging dinosaur wasn't enough trouble, this colossal creature is doubly dangerous as she's a mother on the lookout for whoever swiped her eggs. Now, what was that Sid was saying about starting a new family?

Mamma's coming

This protective parent doesn't believe in keeping her feelings to herself and will stop at nothing to get her kids back.

NEW DADDY

You wouldn't know it to look at him, but Manny, on the brink of fatherhood, is the happiest guy alive. But having a baby on the way has made him even more of a worrier than normal – which his friends probably thought wasn't possible!

Trying to remember how to burp a baby

Baby power
When Manny hears the first cry of his new baby, it gives him that extra bit of determination to survive a terrifying guanlong attack – and be there for his family.

"DON'T OVEREXCITE THE BABY!"

Big worrier
It's tough being the biggest thing on Earth, and having to face the fact that you can't protect your baby from everything. Manny has tried padding trees and sticking snowballs on pointy branches. Ellie has to calm him down and tell him he's overreacting a little. A little? Manny never was one to do things in a small way!

Babysitting

Manny's most recent experience of being a parent came when he looked after human baby, Roshan. How could something with no horns, fangs or claws turn out to be such a handful?

Family secret

A cave painting near Half Peak reveals the sad story of Manny's first family. They were trapped by human hunters and Manny was unable to save them. This loss has made Manny a great worrier and he fears being hurt again.

SCRAT

This sabre-toothed squirrel is the ultimate Ice Age survivor. He will brave any danger as long as he has a precious nut to protect. Avalanche-proof, he has been trapped under ice and stomped by a mammoth. But perhaps most frightening of all was being given the kiss of life by Sid.

Can scent an acorn half a continent away

Fangs act like ice axes when scaling glaciers

Indigestible shell conceals inedible acorn within

Nuts about nuts
Squirrels have a thing about storing nuts away for the winter and this Ice Age version is in a league all of his own. With a single acorn, he once shattered an entire glacier!

Master of Nut-Fu
Scrat has the moves to take down a whole army of piranhas if they try to come between him and his nut. Rumour has it he learnt from the tae-kwon dodos…

It's hard to surprise a scrat, but he's in for a shock when he meets the female of his own species!

Mime artist
Scrat cannot speak, and is forced to point, mime and act out charades to get his message across.

SCRATTE

More glamorous than the male scrat – which, let's face it, isn't difficult – and with a sly sense of humour, scratte, the female sabre-toothed squirrel, is a delightful creature. Unless, of course, she's just run off with your winter food supply…

Ravishing rodent
The female of the scrat species is sleaker and more colourful than the male. And she generally looks less like she's spent most of her life in avalanches and earthquakes, too.

Nuts about you
Bumping into a female of his own species for the first time is enough to make even a scrat lose his grip. Usually unlucky with acorns, maybe the poor scrat will be luckier in love…

Fangs kept sharp for hooking into ice

Scratte survival
Nature has given the scratte a few helpful tricks when it comes to survival. Extra fur stretching from her arms to her legs forms a pair of wings, enabling her to glide. Skinny, with sharp fangs, she also makes a great grappling hook in a crisis.

Fur has lustrous brown highlights

The object of scratte's affections

Soft pads for silent nut-hunting

DID YOU KNOW?
Squirrels eat 800 acorns per year. But scratte would have been content with just one!

51

CRIME SCENE

Prepare to delve into the dark side of animal nature. A strange crime has been committed and only the brilliant mind of detective Buckminster can solve it. A weird collection of clues leads the gang onto the trail of the missing Sid. But this mystery is not for the faint-hearted. The gang can hardly bear to look as Buck discovers something that even he finds truly horrible…broccoli!

Clue 1: On the scent
Buck first stumbles onto the trail when his trusty nose detects a smell like a buzzard's butt fell off and was sprayed on by skunks. Diego explains there's only one guy who could smell as bad as that…Sid!

Veg out
The confused crime scene was created earlier that day when Mamma Dino prepared a meat feast of fresh archaeopteryx, and objected to Sid putting veggies on the menu!

Clue 2: Telltale tuft
Eagle-eyed Buck spots a tuft of fur so rancid it could only come from Sid. Being an expert on survival, surely he should know better than to stick his nose so close to such a hazardous substance?

Clue 4: Sharp sabre
It's lucky that there's a real tracking expert on the scene to help out – the super-sleuthing sabre-tooth, Diego. He spots a row of trees that have all been smashed to bits. Buck concludes that when Sid escaped the food fight he had a new peril to contend with – Rudy was on his trail!

Clue 3: Grizzly remains
Next, Buck finds the most shocking evidence yet…the partly chewed remains of a once-living creature. Thank goodness it isn't Sid! How does Buck know? Because of the broccoli, of course. Sid obviously fought back with it, leaving the poor dinosaur a vegetable.

TEAMWORK

There may be one or two drawbacks to hanging out with the strangest herd ever, but there is one big bonus – teamwork. With their amazing blend of skills, these guys can get out of any scrape. But they also have quite a talent for getting into trouble in the first place!

Having a stinky sloth on your head may not sound a great advantage, but Sid is perfectly placed to give Manny those tundra traffic reports.

"THAT'S WHAT YOU DO IN A HERD. YOU LOOK OUT FOR EACH OTHER."

Right on track
The three amigos proved a great team when it came to tracking down the human tribe and returning baby Roshan. Of course, nobody wants a sabre creeping up behind them, so Manny's message to Diego was very clear: stay up front where I can see you!

Ptero-team

Crash and Eddie make a great crew when Buck pilots a passing pterodactyl. While Buck steers from behind the bird's head, the wily brothers pick fruit off the trees and use it as anti-pterodactyl ammo.

Nasty fingernails for ripping prey

Long tail aids steady flight

DID YOU KNOW? Pterodactyls are not dinosaurs but pterosaurs – winged lizards. The creatures' wing stretches out from its body to a uniquely long finger tip.

Wings made of skin, not feathers

Sharp claws can cling to anything

Give and take

Luckily for Diego, this cliffhanger has a happy ending. With a helping trunk from a good pal, it's amazing what you can achieve. Manny teaches Diego that risking your life to save others is just what you do in a herd.

55

NEW MUMMY

It's a long wait for the happy event, but when her baby finally arrives, Ellie is the happiest mum in the world. Bringing her baby up in a dangerous world isn't going to be half so tough as stopping the rest of the herd from spoiling Peaches rotten.

Mum uses her trunk like an arm to wrap around her precious delivery.

Heavy subject
Ellie is anxious that being pregnant is making her ankles look fat. Manny tactfully points out that he never knew she had any ankles in the first place.

With her cute topknot, Peaches takes after her mum.

Call it mother's intuition – when Sid resists taking the dino eggs back, Ellie is sure that someone will come looking for them.

Special delivery

When Ellie tells Manny, "It's time!", he thinks she means it's time for lunch. Then, when the baby starts to arrive, the herd are attacked by a pack of snapping guanlongs! While Manny defends the herd, Diego is there with a friendly paw for Ellie to hold.

DID YOU KNOW?

Female mammoths were good mothers and liked to stay with their young and keep them safely within a larger herd.

PEACHES

This lovable furball totters out into the world with no idea of the fuss her arrival has caused. But after all the arguments, issues and dramas, Manny's herd have reached a decision. The arrival of a baby is a reason for them all to stay together, not fall apart. Welcome to the Ice Age, Peaches!

Sid gives Peaches the thumbs-up!

Pretty Peaches
Uncle Sid is relieved to see that the new baby takes after her mum with her good looks. No offence to Manny, but his beauty is definitely hidden away on the inside!

DID YOU KNOW?
Baby mammoths fattened up by drinking their mother's milk, just like baby elephants do today.

"SHE'S SWEET AND ROUND AND COVERED WITH FUZZ."

Meet the family
For once, Crash and Eddie show their soft side and get all weepy at the sight of the new family member. They are delighted to discover that Peaches can hang upside down from a tree, just like them!

Mother and daughter both have bright green eyes

New fur is shorter and less shaggy than mum's

Peaches lives up to her name with her sweet smile.

Name game
Manny once told Ellie he loves peaches because they're sweet, round and fuzzy – just like her. He suggests they call the baby Little Ellie, but mum remembers Manny's words and suggests Peaches instead!

FAMILY ALBUM

We all love to look back on those special moments – times that were magical, romantic or sometimes just plain embarrassing. It's nice to recall life's big events – making new friends, taking that big road trip or maybe even having your life saved by a crazy weasel.

"YOU GOT MY RESPECT BUDDY."

Sid and Manny will never forget the moment they became parents for the first time – sort of! Baby Roshan taught them a lot about caring for others and nappy changing.

Mammoth crush

Despite the rows, scowls and cruel personal insults, it was a magic moment when Manny realised that Ellie really cared for him. The tender touch of a trunk can say so much.

Sticking together

After the gang have just escaped being cooked alive by lava, and Manny has recovered from Sid standing on the end of his trunk, it's time for a bit of team-bonding. In a dangerous world you just have to look out for each other.

Enter the weasel

Meeting Buck is an adventure the herd will never forget – if they live to tell the tale. This is a very rare shot of Buck looking cool and relaxed. Usually he is hurling stinky fruit at an ankylosaurus, or holding a conversation with a rock.

Crash and Eddie's lives are one magic moment after another and they spend their time laughing in the face of danger.

Happy family

Family is the people you love and Crash, Eddie and Ellie have an unbreakable bond. It doesn't matter that they are different species'!

HAPPY ENDING

A sparkling ice mobile in a children's playground tells a happy story. Giant dinosaurs, rivers of lava and insecurities may have threatened to break them up, but the herd now face the future together. And with that tempting acorn hanging there too, you can be sure the Scrats will be along at any minute…

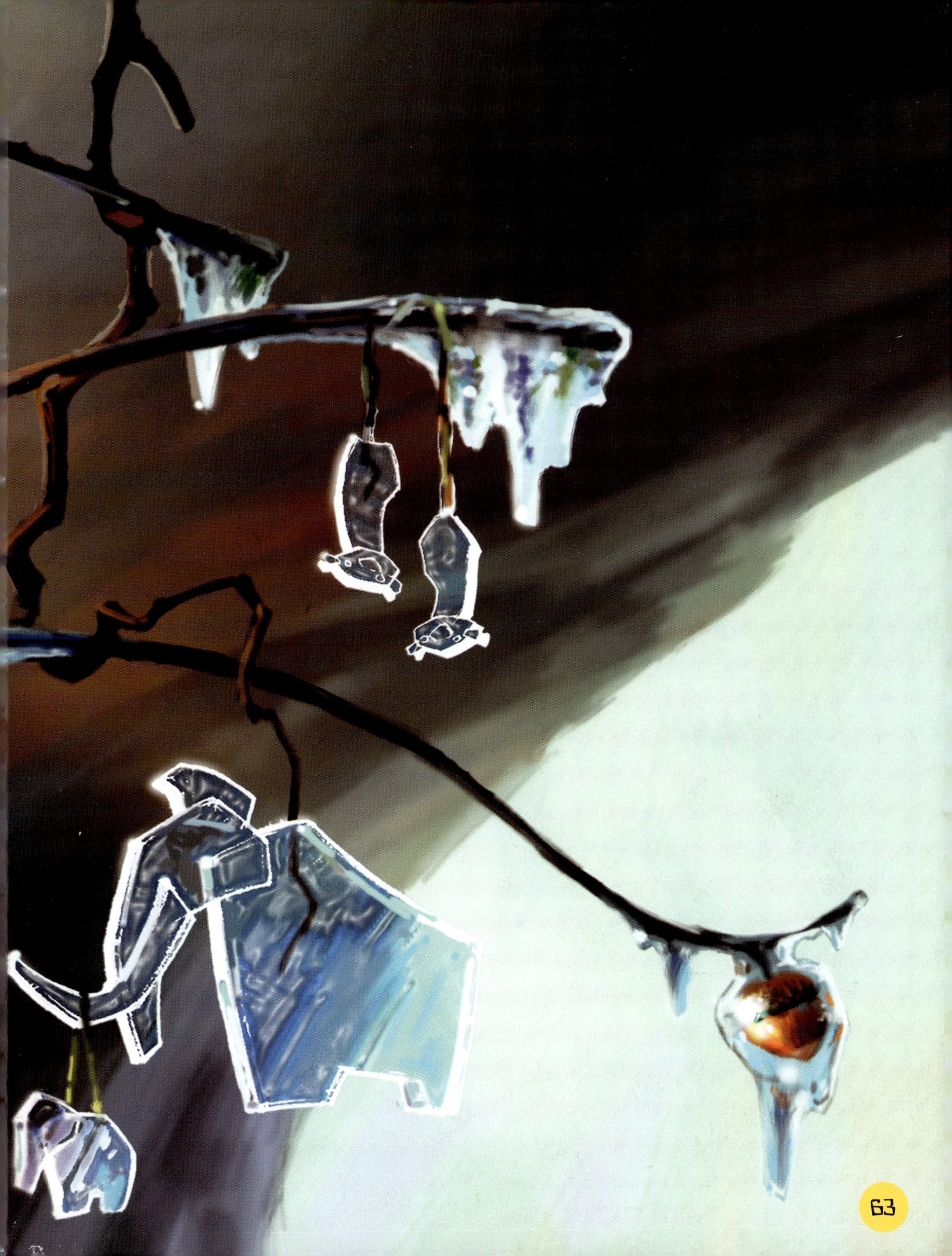

LONDON, NEW YORK, MUNICH,
MELBOURNE, AND DELHI

Editor Jo Casey
Designers Owen Bennett and Julie Thompson
Managing Editor Catherine Saunders
Art Director Lisa Lanzarini
Publishing Manager Simon Beecroft
Category Publisher Alex Allan
Production Editor Sean Daly
Production Controller Nick Seston

First published in Great Britain in 2009 by
Dorling Kindersley Limited,
80 Strand, London, WC2R 0RL

09 10 11 12 13 10 9 8 7 6 5 4 3 2 1
ID082 – 03/09

Copyright © 2009 Twentieth Century Fox Film Corporation
Page design copyright © 2009 Dorling Kindersley Limited

Ice Age, *Ice Age 2: The Meltdown* and *Ice Age 3: Dawn of the Dinosaurs* TM & ©
2009 Twentieth Century Fox Film Corporation. All Rights Reserved.

No part of this publication may be reproduced, stored in a retrieval system,
or transmitted in any form or by any means, electronic, mechanical,
photocopying, recording or otherwise, without prior written
permission of the copyright owner.

Published in the USA by DK Publishing

A CIP catalogue record for this book
is available from the British Library

ISBN: 978-1-40534-115-8

Colour reproduction by MDP in the UK
Printed and bound in China by L. Rex

Discover more at
www.dk.com